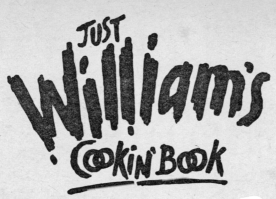

JUST William's Cookin' Book

D1638972

THIS ARMADA BOOK BELONGS TO:

With grateful thanks to Sue Rogers,
Ben, Torti and Matthew

and to London Weekend Television

Just William's Cookin' Book was first published in Armada in 1977
by Fontana Paperbacks, 14 St. James's Place, London SW1A 1PF

Inspired by the William books created and written by Richmal
Crompton.

© Stella Richman Productions Limited 1977.

Printed in Great Britain by Richard Clay (The Chaucer Press), Ltd.,
Bungay, Suffolk.
Typeset by Bedford Typesetters Ltd.

JUST William's Cookin' Book

Written by David Reid
Compiled by Brenda Leys
Designed by Terry Griffiths
Illustrated by Pat Gavin

Armada

CONTENTS

*SEEIN' AS HOW THEY'RE <u>HELPFUL</u> READ 'EM BEFORE YOU BEGIN.

Cookin is REELY VERY Simple.

I DON'T KNOW WHY GROWN-UBS ARE ALWAYS GOIN' ON ABOUT HOW ~~hard~~ DIFFICULT IT is.

ALL YOU GOT TO DO IS BURN A FEW THINGS UP IN THE OVEN TO STOP 'EM BEING RAW AN' HORRID AN' THAT'S COOKIN ISN'T IT?

STILL I GOTTA ADMIT I LIKE SOME THINGS BETTER THAN OTHERS SO ALL YOU GOT TO DO IS FIND OUT WHAT TO DO TO THINGS TO MAKE 'EM TASTE NICE. THAT'S WHAT GROWN-UPS CALL RECEPEES WHICH IS FOREN FOR COOKIN'.

WHY THEY CAN'T SAY COOKIN WHEN THEY MEAN COOKIN I DON'T KNOW. I BET ANYONE CAN COOK ALL THE RECEPEES IN THIS BOOK ANYWAY 'COS THEY'RE ALL EASY 'AN WHATS MORE THEY'RE USEFUL WHEN YOUR **HUNGRY.**

William

COOKIN' OUTSIDE

THINGS YOU CAN COOK OUTSIDE INSEAD OF BORING OLD SITTING ROUND THE TABLE HAVIN YOUR TEA.

First of all you've got to light a fire with wood or charcoal. Make sure you start off with just a small fire otherwise it'll get too big and then everyone'll tell you you're goin' to set the house on fire or something stupid like that. Use things like dead fir cones, paper and twigs to get it started.

When you've got it goin' put some bricks or something down each side and go and borrow a shelf out of the oven so that its' like a grill over the hot fire. You'd better ask if you can borrow the shelf only they're bound to say 'You won't burn yourself, will you?' Try not to say 'Yes' cos this leads to grown-ups not understanding jokes.

SAUSAGE KEBABS

4 helpings

4 sausages   *2 onions*
2 tomatoes   *little oil*
2 mushrooms

Divide each sausage into four. Cut the tomatoes and mushrooms in half. Peel and quarter the onions. With a pastry brush, brush everything with a little oil. Push them on to skewers, mixing up sausage with tomato, mushroom and onion. Lay across the embers of the fire and turn them around several times so they get cooked all over. Remember to hold the ends of the skewers with a thick kitchen cloth.

HAMBURGER DRUMSTICKS

4 helpings

1 lb (450g) minced beef
2 oz (50g) crushed crisps (any flavour)
salt and pepper
1 egg

Mix everything together in a bowl. Take good-sized lumps and squeeze them round the end of a clean stick. Lay over the embers of a bonfire and turn them often until they are cooked all over.

BAKED BEANS AN' TOMATO SOUP

4 helpings

1 *medium tin baked beans*
1 *large onion*
2 *sticks celery*
1 *lb tomatoes*
½ *pint (300ml) water*

¼ *pint (150ml) milk*
salt and pepper
pinch of ground cloves
toast

Peel and chop the onion. Wash and chop the celery, slice the tomatoes. Put them all in a heated saucepan of water and bring to the boil. Simmer gently for 30 minutes. Add the baked beans and stir. Sprinkle in the pepper, salt and cloves and stir in the milk. Serve hot, with toast.

BARBECUE SAUSAGES

4 helpings

1 *lb (450g) pork sausages*
sweet pickle
1 *soft roll for each sausage*

Split open the sausages lengthwise and fill with sweet pickle. Close up and wrap each one tightly in foil. Cook in the embers of the fire for about 20-30 minutes. Take out carefully with tongs, unwrap and put each sausage into a soft roll.

(These can also be cooked in the oven, gas mark 4, electric 350°F (180°C), for about 20 minutes.)

JACKET POTATOES

Scrub and prick the potatoes. Wrap each one tightly in silver foil and bury them in the embers of the fire. They should take about an hour. Serve with butter, cottage cheese, or grated cheese.

IF YOU USE THE SHOE POLISH BRUSH 'STEAD OF THE NAIL BRUSH THEY TASTE ROTTEN

(*For cooking jacket potatoes in the oven, see page 17 .*)

PiGS iN BLANKETS

4-6 helpings

6 frankfurters
mustard
6 rashers streaky bacon

Split the frankfurters, spread them inside with a little mustard and
wrap them tightly round with a slice of bacon. You can cook three
at a time on a long skewer and set them over the embers of a good
bonfire, turning them often until the bacon is sizzly.

DAMPERS

makes about 10-12

1 lb (450g) self-raising flour
pinch of salt
enough water to make a stiff dough

Mix everything together in a bowl, adding the water slowly so that
your dough isn't too 'wet'. Find some long, strong sticks and with a
sharp knife peel off the bark. Take lumps of dough and twirl them
around one end of the stick. Lay them across the top of the embers
of a good bonfire and keep turning them until they are cooked all
over. Lovely filled with butter and jam.

BARBECUE BAKED BEANS

4-6 helpings

1 *tablespoon oil*
1 *onion*
1 *tablespoon tomato ketchup*
1 *tablespoon treacle*

1 *teaspoon mustard*
1 *teaspoon water*
1 *teaspoon Worcester sauce*
1 *very large tin baked beans*

Peel and slice the onion. Heat the oil in a saucepan over a low heat. Fry the onion in the oil until it is soft and transparent. Add the ketchup, treacle, mustard, Worcester sauce and water. Stir it all together and cook for a few minutes. Open the tin of beans and add to the saucepan. Stir it all up and heat until it is nearly boiling.

ROAST CORN COBS

1 *corn cob for each person*
a little butter

Pull the green outer leaves off the corn and remove all the long stringy threads. Brush the butter all over the corn and place on a grid over hot embers. Turn frequently. They take about 15 minutes to cook.

TOASTED MARSHMALLOWS

As many marshmallows as you can eat.

Spear each marshmallow on the end of a long stick. Hold it near the flames or embers until it begins to bubble. Eat at once.

BAKED BANANAS

1 *banana for each person*
2 *oz (50g) butter*
2 *oz (50g) brown sugar*

juice of one lemon
grated rind of one lemon and
one orange

Peel the bananas and slice them in half lengthwise. Spread out a large piece of silver foil and pile the bananas on to it. Add the butter, cut into knobs, sprinkle brown sugar over the top, with the grated rind of the lemon and orange and pour the lemon juice over the bananas. Wrap it all up into a parcel and cook over the hot embers of a bonfire.

Or you can put the bananas, etc, into an oven-proof dish and cook in the oven for 20 minutes at gas mark 4, electric 350°F (180°C).

SNOW ICE CREAM

4 *helpings*

snow
1 *carton single cream*
little castor sugar
vanilla essence

Fill a dish with clean, freshly fallen snow. Stir in some single cream and a little sugar and flavour with a drop of vanilla essence. Put in the ice-making part of the fridge or deep freeze for about an hour.

KITCHEN COOKIN'

THINGS TO COOK IN THE KITCHEN WHEN IT'S RAINING AN' YOU CAN'T LIGHT A FIRE OUTSIDE AN' EVERYBODY'S SAYIN' THINGS LIKE "WHY DON'T YOU DO SOMETHIN' USEFUL 'STEAD OF LOOKIN' FED UP"

USEFUL HINTS

① YOU GOTTA REMEMBER TO BE CLEANER THAN WHEN YOU'RE OUTSIDE. YOU MIGHT AS WELL WASH YOUR HANDS BEFORE YOU START 'COS YOU'LL ONLY BE TOLD TO ALL THE TIME.

② THE OTHER THING THEY'RE ALWAYS GOIN' ON ABOUT IS WASHIN' UP. PERSONALLY I DON'T AGREE WITH IT. WHY YOU GOT TO CLEAN UP A SAUCEPAN WHEN YOU'RE ONLY GOIN' TO COOK SOMETHING IN IT TOMORROW. I DON'T UNDERSTAND BUT THERE'S NO CONVINCING THEM.

THEY'LL GO ON AN' ON AN' ON AT YOU 'BOUT THE WASHIN' UP SO DON'T SAY YOU HAVEN'T BEEN WARNED. 'NOTHER THING I DISCOVERD IS I THOUGHT IT'D BE QUICKER JUST TO RUN THE WATER OVER THINGS AN' WIPE 'EM ONLY, BUT IT TURNED OUT TO BE FASTER TO USE THE WASHIN' UP STUFF AN' DO IT, WHAT THEY CALL PROPERLY. (TURNED OUT THEY WERE RIGHT, BUT I DIDN'T SAY SO.)

14

BAKED BREAD OMELETTE

4-6 *helpings*

6 oz (175g) *stale bread without the crusts*
5 *eggs*
½ oz (12g) *parsley*
¼ oz (6g) *thyme*

Cover bread with boiling water and leave it to soak for about an hour. Turn oven on to gas mark 2, electric 300°F (150°C). Drain off any remaining water from the bread and mash it with a fork, adding the chopped parsley and thyme and the salt and pepper. In a separate bowl, break the eggs and beat well. Mix in with the bread, put into an ovenproof dish and cook in the middle of the oven for about an hour.

POTATO PANCAKES

4 *helpings*

3 *large potatoes*
2 *eggs*
2 *tablespoons milk*
3 *tablespoons flour*

¼ *teaspoon baking powder*
1 *teaspoon salt*
1 *small onion*
pinch of pepper

Peel the potatoes. Grate the potatoes into a bowl of cold water. Squeeze the potatoes to get the water out of them and put them into a clean bowl. Peel and grate the onion and add it to the potato.

Beat the eggs together with the milk, salt and pepper and mix into the potato/onion mixture. Also stir in the flour and baking powder. Heat a little oil or butter in a frying pan. Drop teaspoons of the pancake mixture into the frying pan and fry until golden brown on both sides.

SPARE RIBS

4 *helpings*

1 *lb* (450g) *spare rib pork chops*
1 *jar mustard*
4 *oz* (100-125g) *soft brown sugar*

Heat the oven to medium, gas mark 4, electric 350°F (180°C). Lay the chops in an oven-proof dish big enough to hold them all side by side. Mix together the mustard and brown sugar in a bowl. Spoon the mixture all over the chops, making sure they are all covered. Bake in the oven for 40 minutes to an hour. You can eat them in your fingers, holding the ends with a paper towel.

MEAT LOAF

4 *helpings*

1 *lb* (450g) *minced beef*
1 *small tin tomatoes*
1 *packet sage and onion stuffing*
pinch of mixed herbs

tomato ketchup
brown sauce (eg H.P.)
dash of Worcester sauce
salt and pepper

Turn the oven on to gas mark 4, electric 350°F (180°C). In a mixing bowl put the mince, sage and onion stuffing, tomatoes, mixed herbs, a good splash of brown sauce, a dash of Worcester sauce and a sprinkle of salt and pepper. Mix everything together with a big fork very thoroughly. Grease a loaf tin and pile the mixture into it, smoothing over the top with a knife. Pour lots of tomato ketchup over the top and cook it in the middle of the oven for one hour. You can eat this hot or leave it until it is cold and cut it into slices.

JACKET POTATOES

Choose large firm potatoes. Scrub them with a nail brush under the cold tap. Stab them about three times with a fork and put them at the very top of the oven for 45 minutes at the highest setting (as hot as you can). At the end of this time, turn the oven down to the lowest possible setting and let them cook for another 15 minutes. Cooked this way the skins are really nice to eat too. Serve them split open with a big knob of butter, and salt and pepper.

BUBBLE AN' SQUEAK

4 *helpings*

1 *lb (or whatever there is) of cold mashed potato and any cold left-over greens like sprouts or peas*

Mix everything together in a bowl with a sprinkle of salt and pepper. (You can add some grated cheese too, if you like.) Put a frying pan on the cooker and over a gentle heat melt some fat. (Bacon fat is best, but any dripping will do). Scoop in the potato mixture and press it well down with the back of a fish slice. Let it fry gently for about 7 minutes, then turn it over and fry the other side. Serve it quickly.

PARCEL POST

This is the easiest way to cook a complete dinner all-in-one.

4 helpings

4 lean lamb chops
4 large tomatoes
4 large potatoes
½ oz (12g) margarine or butter

Turn on the oven to gas mark 5, electric 375°F (190°C). Cut four big squares of silver foil and spread them out on the table. Put a lamb chop in the centre of each foil square. Cut each tomato into three or four slices and put them on top of the chops. Peel the potatoes, cut each one into thin slices and put these over the tomatoes. Sprinkle a little salt and pepper over the top and carefully wrap up the parcels so that they are sealed. Place them on a baking sheet and put into the oven for 1 hour. Lift them out and open them very carefully as hot steam will come out. Spread them on plates and serve.

These parcels can also be cooked in a bonfire.

FRIED SANDWICHES

left-over slices of any cooked meat   salt and pepper
mashed potatoes   handful of breadcrumbs
1 egg

Spread a layer of mashed potato over each side of a thin piece of cooked meat. Break the egg on to a plate and stir with a fork until it's mixed. Put the breadcrumbs on a separate plate. Dip the 'sandwich' on both sides first in the egg, and then in the breadcrumbs. Put some oil or dripping in a frying pan on the cooker and fry the 'sandwiches' on both sides until brown and crispy.

SARDINES AN' HONEY

2 helpings

1 slice of hot buttered toast for   1 tablespoon tomato ketchup
  each person   1 tablespoon Worcester sauce
1 tin sardines in tomato sauce   1 teaspoon mustard
1 tablespoon honey

Open the tin of sardines and pour the contents into a bowl. Add all the other ingredients and mash up with a fork. Spread on hot buttered toast and put under a hot grill for 3 minutes.

ROWLEYS

4 helpings

1 lb (450g) sausage meat   salt and pepper
1 teaspoon mixed herbs   some oil or fat for frying
2 oz (50g) flour

Break off small pieces of sausage meat and roll them into little balls in your hands. On a plate, mix the flour with the herbs, salt and pepper and roll each of the 'Rowleys' in it until they are covered. Gently heat a frying pan with enough oil to cover the bottom and drop the Rowleys in, turning them over gently as they fry until they are brown all over. Eat hot or cold.

SARDINE CRISP

2-3 helpings

4 *slices bread*
1 *tin sardines*
2 *oz (50g) cheddar cheese*

2 *tablespoons breadcrumbs*
2 *tablespoons milk*
pinch of salt and pepper

Grate the cheese into a bowl and stir in the breadcrumbs, milk, salt and pepper. Turn on the grill and toast the bread on both sides. Drain the oil away from the sardines and lift them carefully out and put them on the hot toast. Spread the cheese mixture on to the sardines and put them back under the grill for about 3 minutes.

CHEESE CRUMPETS

3 helpings

6 *crumpets*
butter
6 *slices cheese*

Grill the crumpets—brown side (the side without holes) first. Put a slice of cheese on each holey side, after you have buttered it, and pop it back under the grill until the cheese has melted and started to turn brown.

APPLE DUMPLINGS

4 helpings

7 oz (200g) plain flour
pinch of salt
4 oz (100-125g) margarine and
  lard mixed
water to mix

4 good-sized apples
2 oz (50g) sugar
a little milk
a little castor sugar

Turn the oven on to gas mark 7, electric 425°F (220°C). Sieve the flour and salt into a mixing bowl. Add the margarine and lard cut into small knobs and rub in with the fingertips until the mixture looks like breadcrumbs. Add the water slowly and mix with a knife to make a good soft dough. Divide this into four pieces. On a board sprinkled with flour, roll each piece out and cut into a 15 cm circle using a small plate as a guide.

Peel and core the apples and place one on each circle, filling up the centre of the apple with sugar and 1 teaspoon of water. Moisten the edges of the pastry with water and carefully gather them to the top of the apple and press firmly together.

Grease a baking sheet, turn the dumplings upside down on to it and bake in the middle of the oven for 10 minutes. Turn the oven down to gas mark 3, electric 325°F (170°C), and cook for another 30 minutes. Take out and sprinkle castor sugar over the top before serving.

BREAD PUDDING

8 helpings

½ *lb* (225g) *bread*	2 *oz* (50g) *raisins*
3 *oz* (75g) *sugar*	¼ *pint* (150ml) *milk*
1 *egg*	*pinch of grated nutmeg*
2 *oz* (50g) *currants*	*grated rind of one lemon*

Put the bread in a bowl and cover with cold water. Leave it to soak for about an hour. Turn the oven on to gas mark 4, electric 350°F (180°C). Drain all the water off and squeeze the bread in your fingers to get out as much of the water as possible. Add all the other ingredients and mix very thoroughly with a wooden spoon. Grease a roasting tin and scrape the mixture into it. Cook in the middle of the oven for an hour.

BAKED APPLES

1 *large Bramley apple for each person*	1 *knob of butter for each apple*
1 *tablespoon runny honey for each apple*	*some brown sugar* *a few sultanas or raisins*

Remove the core from the apples and place them side by side in an oven-proof dish. Into the hole left by the core pour brown sugar, and a few raisins. Pour the honey over the top and dot each apple with a knob of butter. Put them in a medium oven gas mark 4, electric 350°F (180°C) for 40 minutes.

CHOCARINA

1 *choc ice*
2 *tablespoons orange marmalade*
2 *tablespoons orange squash*

Put the marmalade and orange squash into a saucepan and bring it to the boil. Cut the choc ice diagonally in half and pour the sauce over the top. Serve at once.

FIVE MINUTE PUDDING

4 helpings

3 *tablespoons flour*
3 *dessertspoons sugar*
2 *eggs*

1 *dessertspoon baking powder*
jam

Turn oven on to gas mark 4, electric 350°F (180°C). Mix everything, except the jam, in a bowl, beating with a fork to remove any lumps. Pour the mixture into a greased baking tin. Put it in the oven for 5 minutes. Take out of the oven, spread jam all over the top, and with a spoon roll it up like a Swiss roll. Carefully lift it out of the tin and serve.

TEA CAKES

(This is truly a tea cake, as it's made with cold tea!)

1 *lb (450g) mixed fruit*
  (sultanas, raisins, currants, peel)
1 *mug of brown sugar*
1 *mug of cold tea (without milk)*

1 *beaten egg*
2 *mugs of self-raising flour*

Put the mixed fruit, the brown sugar and the cold tea into a bowl. Leave it to stand overnight. Next day add the beaten egg and the flour and stir well. Heat the oven to gas mark 4, electric 350°F (180°C). Put the cake mixture into two greased loaf tins and cook in the middle of the oven for one hour. This is delicious left for a few days and then eaten sliced and spread with butter.

SPONGE CAKE AN' BUTTER ICING

2 eggs
2 oz (50g) *castor sugar*
2 oz (50g) *self-raising flour*

Turn on the oven to gas mark 5, electric 375°F (190°C). In a mixing bowl whisk the eggs and sugar together until light and creamy. Sieve the flour into the mixture and stir in with a fork. Grease an 8 inch (20 cm) sandwich tin and pour the mixture into it. Put in the middle of the oven for 12-14 minutes. When it's cooked, leave it in the tin for a few minutes before turning it out. Leave to get cold. Then carefully cut it in half horizontally with a sharp knife, so that you have two round thin cakes. Sandwich them together with BUTTER ICING.

BUTTER ICING

4 oz (125g) *butter*
5 oz (150g) *icing sugar*

Sieve the icing sugar into a bowl and add the butter cut into small knobs. Mix these together with a fork until you have a thick creamy mixture. Flavour it if you like:-

Chocolate   *2 teaspoons cocoa or 2 tablespoons drinking chocolate or 2 oz (50g) melted chocolate.*

Lemon   *2 teaspoons very finely grated lemon rind and 2 dessertspoons lemon juice.*

Coconut   *2 oz (50g) dessicated coconut.*

Coffee   *2 dessertspoons Camp coffee or 2 teaspoons instant coffee dissolved in 4 teaspoons hot water.*

CRISPY CRACKLY CAKE

1 oz (25g) sugar
1 oz (25g) butter
1 oz (25g) cocoa

1 tablespoon golden syrup
1 oz (25g) cornflakes or
   rice crispies

Put the sugar, butter, cocoa and golden syrup into a saucepan. Put the pan on a low heat and melt them together very slowly, stirring all the time with a wooden spoon so they do not stick to the bottom. When they are all melted together take the pan off the heat and leave it to cool for 5 minutes. Then stir in the cornflakes or rice crispies until they are all covered with the chocolate mixture. Then spread them all over a large plate and put in the fridge to set.

FLAPJACKS

4 oz (100-125g) margarine
3 oz (75g) sugar
2 tablespoons golden syrup
pinch of salt

handful of raisins, currants
   or sultanas
4 oz (100-125g) rolled oats
   (porridge oats)

Turn on the oven to gas mark 4, electric 350°F (180°C). Heat the margarine in a saucepan until it melts. Then stir in the sugar, golden syrup, salt, raisins and lastly the oats. Take the pan off the heat and mix everything well together. Grease a baking sheet and spread the mixture over it. Don't worry if it doesn't reach the edges as it spreads a bit while cooking. Put the tin in the middle of the oven for 15-20 minutes. Mark into squares with a knife while still hot in the tin and leave to cool before lifting them out.

COOKIN' FOR DYIN' PEEPLE

WHAT TO DO WHEN ALL YOUR FAMILY BREAK OUT IN SPOTS AN' BECOME INVALIDS ALL OF A SUDDEN. 'STEAD OF SAYIN' SENSIBLE THINGS TO YOU LIKE "GO AWAY FROM US. AS FAR AS YOU CAN OR YOU MIGHT CATCH WHAT WE'VE GOT," THEY EXPECT YOU TO DO THINGS FOR THEM AN' HANG AROUND THEM AN' RUN DREDFUL RISKS. JUST 'COS THEY'RE LYING IN BED BEIN' ILL AN' NOT GETTIN' UP IN THE MORNING THEY DON'T THINK ABOUT HOW ILL YOU'RE GOIN' TO FEEL IF YOU DO CATCH WHATEVER IT IS THEY'VE GOT. ALL THEY WANT IS FOR YOU TO COOK THEM THEIR BREAKFAST AND KART IT ALL THE WAY UP TO THEM.

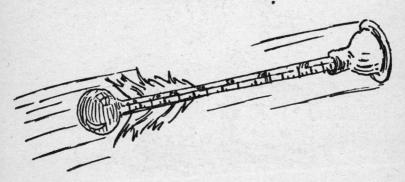

SCRAMBLED EGGS

2 helpings

3 eggs
yoghurt pot of milk (5fl oz, 150ml)
salt and pepper
knob of butter

Break the eggs into a bowl. Add milk and salt and pepper. Whisk up with a fork or an egg whisk until smooth and creamy. Heat a knob of butter in a saucepan. When the butter is melted (don't let it turn brown) pour in the egg mixture and stir all the time until the eggs begin to set and scramble. Serve at once on hot buttered toast.

PLAIN OMELETTE

These quantities make an omelette for one person.

2 eggs
1 tablespoon cold water
little salt and pepper
butter

Break the eggs into a bowl, add the water and a sprinkle of salt and pepper. Beat hard with a fork for about a minute. Heat a knob of butter in a frying pan. When it is sizzling, pour in the egg mixture, gently tilting the pan from side to side so that the mixture covers the bottom. Stir it gently with a fork. When it is set, fold it in half with a spatula or slice and slide on to a plate.

BACON OMELETTE

1 bacon rasher for each person
1 egg for each person
½ oz (12g) margarine or butter
salt and pepper

Cut off the bacon rind, slice the bacon into small pieces and fry them in a frying pan until they are crisp. Add the butter and, while it melts, break the egg into a bowl, add the salt and pepper and whisk it up with a fork. Pour the egg mixture over the bacon and shake the pan gently around so that the bottom is covered. When it is all set, fold it in half in the pan with a spatula or slice and slide it out on to a plate.

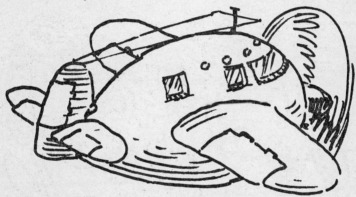

WHIRLPOOL POACHED EGGS

1 egg per person
salt
vinegar
1 slice of buttered toast per person

Bring half a saucepan full of water to the boil. Turn it to simmer. Add two pinches of salt and a tiny drop of vinegar. Break an egg into a cup. Take a fork and stir the simmering water until you have made a whirlpool in the centre. Pour the egg quickly into the middle of the whirlpool. The swirling water will keep the egg together. When the white of the egg starts to set, scoop the egg carefully out of the water with a spatula or slice and serve on buttered toast.

NURRISHN SOUP

6-8 helpings

1 or 2 each of any vegetables. A good mix would be:

2 leeks	salt and pepper
2 carrots	Worcester sauce
2 potatoes	water
2 onions	1 oz (25g) butter
2 stock cubes	

Wash, peel and chop up the vegetables into small chunks. In a really large saucepan melt the butter and add all the vegetables. Stir them round with a big wooden spoon. Add the stock cubes and enough water to generously cover the vegetables (about 4 milk bottles full). Turn up the heat until it comes to the boil. Add the salt, pepper and a dash of Worcester sauce. Turn down the heat and let it simmer for about an hour. You can serve it just as it is, or push it all through a sieve into a clean saucepan or put it in an electric blender.

iNVALiD'S JELLY

4 helpings

1 *packet jelly (any flavour)*
¾ *pint (400ml) water and milk (half and half)*

Break up the jelly into a bowl. Heat half the milk and water in a saucepan and pour on to the jelly pieces. Stir until the jelly has dissolved. Pour on the other half of the milk and water, stir and pour into little bowls or cups. Put in the fridge to set.

APPLE SNOW

4 helpings

3 *eating apples*
1 *tablespoon sugar*   1 *egg*
2 *tablespoons water*   *juice of half a lemon*

Peel the apples, cut them into quarters and carefully cut out the core. Cut them into small pieces. Put them into a saucepan with the sugar and the water. Put the saucepan on a low heat and cook for a few minutes until the apple is soft and mushy. Take off the cooker and whisk up the apple with a fork. Separate the egg yolk from the white, and whisk up the white in a bowl until it is fluffy and snowy. Squeeze out the juice of the lemon. Gently stir the apple and lemon juice into the beaten egg white and mix it all up with a fork. Put it into the fridge for a little while to get nice and cold.

BUNNIES ON THE LAWN

6-8 *helpings*

1 *packet of green jelly*
1 *tin pear halves*
$\frac{1}{4}$ *pint (150ml) double cream*

a few halves of peeled almonds
a few chocolate buttons

Make up the green jelly following the instructions on the packet. When it is set, scrape it on to a large flat dish and fork it up so that it looks rough. Drain the juice from the tin of pears and arrange the pear halves (cut side down), on the green jelly 'lawn'. Whip the double cream with an egg whisk until it is really thick and put a blob at the back of each pear 'bunny' for a tail. Stick two almond halves on the front for ears, and two chocolate drops for eyes.

STAR APPLES

Did you know that if you cut an apple in half *crossways*, instead of from the stalk downwards, in the centre of each half there is a star?

Especially nice is to sprinkle each half with sugar and put it under the grill for a few moments.

BLACKBERRY JUNKET

Everyone knows about blackberry and apple pies and bramble jelly but here is a really delicious way of cooking blackberries which is very, very easy.

Squash blackberries in a nylon sieve and let all the juice come through. When you've got a good bowlful of the juice, leave it to stand in a warm room overnight. Do not stir it, or add anything at all to it. In the morning it will have set lightly and should be eaten with cream and sweet biscuits.

YOGHURT ICECREAM

4 (5fl oz, 150ml) pots plain yoghurt
½ oz (12g) gelatine
2 oz (50g) sugar
1 15 oz (425g) tin raspberries or strawberries

Drain the juice from the tin of fruit into a jug. Put the powdered gelatine in a cup and stand it in a saucepan of hot water. Add 2 tablespoons of the fruit juice to the gelatine and stir until it has dissolved. In a bowl mix the yoghurt with the fruit, sugar and dissolved gelatine until it's a smooth creamy mixture. Put it in the ice-making part of the fridge or in the deep freeze. After about 3 hours it will be good and mushy, so take it out and whisk it hard with an egg whisk. Put it back to freeze for 2 or 3 hours.

FOOD FOR EATIN'
IN BED

'SPOSIN YOU DO CATCH WHATEVER IT WAS ALL THE REST OF YOUR FAMILY HAD GOT. YOU'LL SUDDENLY FIND YOU'RE IN BED AN' THEY'RE ALL UP AN' ABOUT AN' OFF PLAYIN' TENNIS AN' THINGS LIKE THAT.

So ITS JUST AS WELL TO MAKE SURE YOU KNOW WHAT YOU WANT THEM TO COOK YOU SEEING AS HOIN IT WAS THEIR FAULT THAT YOU'RE ILL IN THE FIRST PLACE.

'COURSE THEY'LL ALL THINK THEY KNOW WHAT'S BEST FOR YOU BUT IF YOU CAN MAKE 'EM BELIEVE YOU'RE REALLY GOIN' TO DIE THEN THEY'LL PROBABLY GIVE YOU WHAT YOU ASK FOR EVEN THOUGH ALL THEY'RE REALLY WAITIN' FOR IS TO MAKE OFF WITH YOUR POCKET MONEY AS SOON AS YOUR DEAD.

WHEN YOU'RE REALLY FEELIN BETTER AN' EVERYONE'S GLAD YOU'RE NOT GOIN TO DIE AFTER ALL YOU COULD ASK FOR JUST 'BOUT ANYTHING YOU LIKE.

CHOCOLATE ICE CREAM

10 *helpings*

5 *fl oz (150ml) milk*
2 *oz (50g) castor sugar*
2 *eggs*

½ *pint (10fl oz 300 ml) double cream*
2 *oz (50g) melted chocolate*

Heat the milk and sugar together in a saucepan but do not boil. Beat the eggs in a bowl and pour the milk and sugar over them. Return the mixture to the saucepan and heat very gently until it becomes thick and creamy. Do not let it boil or you will have scrambled egg ice-cream. Pour it all into a bowl and stir in the melted chocolate. Whip up the cream with an egg whisk until quite thick. When the milk, sugar and egg mixture is cool, mix in the cream with a fork. Put the mixture into the ice-making part of the fridge or in the freezer. When it is frozen and rather mushy (about 1-2 hours) take it out and whisk it up thoroughly again. Put it back in the fridge or freezer until completely frozen.

CINNAMON TOAST

An old-fashioned tea-time treat.

2 oz (50g) *castor sugar*
3 *teaspoons ground cinnamon*
hot buttered toast (4 slices)

In a bowl mix the cinnamon with the sugar. Spread it all over the hot buttered toast and put it back under the grill for a few moments only. Eat at once.

ORANGE FRUIT SALAD

1 *large orange for each person*   *castor sugar*
1 *small apple for each person*   *ice-cream*
3 *grapes for each person*

Cut the top off the orange and scoop out about half the pulp with a spoon. Peel and core the apple and chop up small. Cut each grape in half and take out the seeds. Mix all this fruit in a bowl with the sugar and stuff back into the hollow orange. Put a blob of ice-cream on top and serve at once.

MARVELLOUS ICE CREAM SAUCE

Covers a family size block of ice-cream

This is quite the easiest way to make everyone think you are a brilliant cook.

Put a Mars Bar in a saucepan, and stir it over a low heat. It melts into a lovely thick chocolatey, caramel sauce. Pour it over vanilla ice-cream and eat.

YOGHURT WHIP

4-6 *helpings*

1 *fruit-flavoured jelly*
¾ *pint (400ml) hot water*
4 *oz (100g) fresh fruit (chopped apple, grapes, strawberries, etc.)*
2 *pots plain yoghurt*

Dissolve the jelly in the hot water. Leave it in a cool place to nearly set. Then with an egg whisk, whisk it all up and stir in the fruit and yoghurt and whisk again. Pile into glasses and leave it to set completely.

CHOCOLATE MOUSSE

1 *oz (25g) plain chocolate for each person*
1 *egg for each person*
1 *tablespoon black coffee for each person*
1 *oz butter for each person*

Break the chocolate into squares and put it in a saucepan with the coffee. Put the pan on the cooker over a very low heat and stir all the time until the chocolate has melted. Take off the heat and stir in the butter. Separate the yolk from the white of the egg. When the chocolate mixture has cooled a bit (about 15 minutes) beat in the egg yolk. Whisk the white until it is thick and snowy and stir the chocolate into it, mixing it very thoroughly together. Pour it into little pots or glasses and leave in the fridge for a few hours to set.

COOKIN' FOR TRAMPS

THIS IS THE SORT OF FOOD TRAMPS PROBABLY GET TO EAT IF THEY'RE LUCKY. IF THE GROWN-UPS TELL YOU THEY DON'T WANT YOU TO BE A TRAMP WHEN YOU GROW UP, TELL 'EM YOU'RE GOIN' FOR A PICNIC- ITS THE SAME SORT OF FOOD REALLY ONLY THEY THINK PICNIC SOUNDS NICER. (AND it's GOOD PRACTICE IN CASE YOU DO BECOME A TRAMP).

OPEN SANDWICHES

These are lovely for picnics (although difficult to carry!) and ideal for tea in the garden. The best thing is to invent sandwiches for yourself, depending on what you can find in the larder or fridge, but here are some suggestions.

Butter each slice of bread (or French bread cut down the middle is even better) and lay on it:

1. Sliced hard-boiled egg and 2 anchovy fillets.
2. Mashed sardine topped with tomato ketchup.
3. A slice of ham, a little sweet pickle and a slice of cheese.
4. A slice of ham with half a sliced peach on top.
5. A lettuce leaf, topped with 2 rashers of crisply-fried bacon and 2 slices of tomato.
6. Cold scrambled egg with a chopped spring onion on top.
7. Grated carrot mixed with grated cheese with 2 slices of cucumber on top.
8. Sliced banana with a few raisins, sprinkled all over with brown sugar.

STONEAGE EGGS

Hard-boil some eggs by placing them in a saucepan of cold water, bringing them to the boil and letting them boil for 10 minutes. Run the pan under the cold tap for a few minutes. Boil 2 tea bags in a fresh saucepan of water. Tap the eggs all over with a spoon until the shells are covered with cracks, then put them in the pan with the water and tea bags. Boil them all together, gently, for 10 minutes. When you peel the eggs they will have a lovely design all over them, and you can tell your friends they are really thousands of years old.

TORPEDOES

These are very good on picnics.

Take a crusty roll and cut it in half. Scoop most of the bread out of the bottom half and some from the top half. You can then fill them up with any mixture of things you like. For instance:

    hard-boiled egg and sardines
    sliced tomatoes and mango chutney
    grated carrot and grated cheese
    cold sausage and baked beans
    sliced banana, grated apple and raisins.

Pop the top half back on when you have filled them and wrap each one tightly in foil.

HOT CHEESE ROLLS

1 *roll for each person*   *butter*
4 *oz (100-125g) grated cheese*   *drop of milk*
1 *tablespoon sweet pickle*

Cut the rolls in half. Butter each half. Put the grated cheese, the pickle and about 2 tablespoons of milk in a bowl. Mix this all up with a fork and spread it on the buttered rolls. Put under the grill for a few minutes until bubbly and golden brown.

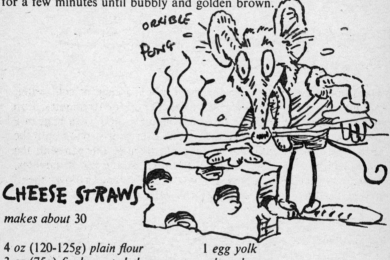

CHEESE STRAWS

makes about 30

4 *oz (120-125g) plain flour*   1 *egg yolk*
3 *oz (75g) finely grated cheese*   *salt and pepper*
2 *oz (50g) butter or margarine*   *cayenne pepper*

Turn oven on to gas mark 6, electric 400°F (200°C). Break the egg and separate the yolk from the white. Sieve the flour into a bowl and add a good pinch of salt and pepper and a good pinch (but not too much) of cayenne pepper. Cut the butter into small knobs and add to the flour with the grated cheese. With your fingertips, rub them into the flour until the mixture looks like breadcrumbs. Add the egg yolk and mix it all to a stiff paste with the blade of a knife. Shape it into a ball with your hands. Roll out the pastry on to a floured board to make a strip about 2½ inches (6 cm) wide and ¼ inch (½ cm) thick. Cut it into strips about ¼ inch (½ cm) wide with a knife. Place the straws on a greased baking sheet and put into the oven for 15-20 minutes or until pale gold in colour. Take out of the oven and leave to cool.

ELDERFLOWER FRITTERS

Pick the heads of the flowers by the stalk and make sure they haven't got insects on them! Don't wash them or you will lose some of the very special flavour.

elderflower heads
4 tablespoons flour
1 egg
1½ cups water

Make the batter as for pancakes (see page 75) but using water instead of milk. Dip the elderflowers into the batter, holding them by the stalk. Have a frying pan with some hot oil in it, already on the cooker. Quickly toss the flowers in the oil until they are brown and crisp. Dust them over with castor sugar and eat.

HAWTHORN SURPRISE

The hawthorn is sometimes called Bread and Cheese tree, although it doesn't taste at all like bread and cheese. The young leaves, picked in April and May taste deliciously nutty.

DANDELION SANDWICH/SALAD

Like hawthorn, much nicer and more interesting to have in salads than boring old lettuce, and you can pick dandelion leaves just about any time of the year.

Try *dandelion sandwiches* with a splash of Worcester sauce. Or fry them lightly in a saucepan with 1 oz (25g) of butter.

DANDELION FLOWERS AN' BACON

quite a few dandelions
streaky bacon

Fry some streaky bacon until it is really crispy and serve it on a plate on which you have spread young dandelion leaves. Make a dressing using a little vinegar, the fat from the bacon and a spot of salt and pepper. Decorate with some of the yellow dandelion flowers—which you should eat as well.

THIS IS A REELY GOOD WAY TO MAKE PEEPLE THINK YOU'RE TRYING TO POISON THEM SO'S THEY'LL ROLL ABOUT IN AGONY FOR DAYS. THEY PROBABLY WON'T EAT IT WHICH IS THEY'RE OWN DAFT FAULT 'COS IT TASTES GOOD

STINGING NETTLE

EVERYONE WILL THINK YOU ARE QUITE MAD WHEN YOU INVITE THEM TO A NETTLE TEA PARTY, BUT THE NETTLES DO NOT STING ONCE THEY ARE COOKED, BEST TO PICK 'EM WEARING GLOVES, THOUGH — AN' NEVER BOTHER TO PICK 'EM AFTER ABOUT JUNE AS THEY WILL BY THEN BE RATHER TOUGH TO EAT.

NETTLES INSTEAD OF CABBAGE

Remove the tough stems, and wash the rest under the cold tap. Just cover the bottom of the saucepan with about ¼ inch of water put the nettles in and boil them with the lid on for about 10 minutes. Strain them well and add a knob of butter. Chop up some spring onions and stir them in.

NETTLE TOAST

Cook some nettles as before. Fry some streaky bacon in a pan until really crispy. Chop it up and mix with the cooked nettles. Spread the mixture on hot-buttered toast, sprinkle with a tablespoon of grated cheese and pop under the grill for a few moments to melt and brown the cheese.

COOKIN' AS PRESENTS

THINGS TO COOK TO GIVE PEEPLE
AS PRESENTS SO'S YOU DON'T HAVE
TO SPEND ALL YOUR POCKET MONEY
ON 'EM. IT'S AMAZIN' HOW
PLEESED GROWN-UPS SEEM TO BE
IF YOU GIVE 'EM SOMETHING TO EAT
THAT YOU'VE COOKED FOR THEIR
BIRTHDAYS AN' CHRISTMAS. PERSONALLY
I'D RATHER HAVE A CRICKET SET OR
A FOOTBALL BUT GROWN-UPS DON'T
SEEM TO MIND, IN FACT THEY
USUALLY SAY, "AREN'T YOU CLEVER"
AN' PAT YOU ON THE HEAD AN'
SOPPY THINGS LIKE THAT.

PEPPERMINT CREAMS

1 lb (450g) icing sugar   makes 1 lb (450g)
1 egg
½ a lemon
peppermint essence

Sieve the icing sugar into a bowl. Separate the egg yolk and white, and put the white in the bowl with the icing sugar. Pound it all together with a wooden spoon. Best of all, knead it all together with your hands. It should be a nice soft lump. If it is dry and crumbly, add a little drop of lemon juice. Slowly add about half a teaspoon of peppermint essence (more if you like them really minty). Press the mixture on to a board with your fingers and cut into small squares. Leave in the fridge to set.

MARZIPAN DATES

½ lb (225g) marzipan   makes about 1 lb (450g)
1 box dates
a little icing sugar

With a pointed knife, carefully slit down the middle of each date and take out the stone. Make little knobs of marzipan with your fingers and put one inside each date. Roll the stuffed dates in icing sugar.

COCONUT ICING

1 lb (450g) sugar lumps
¼ pint (150ml) milk
5 oz (150g) dessicated coconut
cochineal

Grease a shallow, square tin by rubbing with butter, or butter paper. Put the sugar lumps into a saucepan and add the milk. Cook over a gentle heat and stir all the time until the sugar is dissolved. Boil the milk and sugar mixture very carefully, so that it doesn't boil over, for 10 minutes. Stir in the coconut and pour half the mixture into the greased tin so that it spreads all over. Add a few drops of cochineal to the rest of the mixture and stir until it's all pink, then pour it on to the rest in the tin. Smooth over the top with the back of the spoon and leave it in the fridge to set.

NUTTY TOFFEE

makes about 2 lb (900g)

2 *lb (900g) sugar*
8 *fl oz (200ml) golden syrup*
1 *pint (600ml) water*

2 *lb (900g) unsalted peanuts*
  (or walnuts)
2 *level teaspoons bicarbonate*
  of soda
1 *oz (25g) butter*

Put a saucepan on a medium heat and into it put the sugar, golden syrup and water. Stir until the sugar is dissolved, then turn up the heat and boil it, stirring all the time until it forms a thin thread when dropped from the bowl of a spoon. Take the pan off the heat and quickly stir in the nuts, soda and butter. Mix all together. Grease a large flat baking sheet and spread the mixture evenly all over it. Put it in a cold place to set. Then break it up and store it in tins or jars.

FROSTY FRUITS

Any fruit you want to use: grapes and plums are very good and pieces of orange or shelled walnuts or almonds.
1 *egg*
castor sugar

Separate the yolk from the white of the egg. Beat the white in a bowl until it is frothy. Put a good layer of castor sugar on a plate. Twirl each piece of fruit in the egg white until it is covered and then roll it in the castor sugar. Have ready a large plate covered with a piece of silver foil and lay the fruit on this. Put in a cool place to set. These should be eaten within a day or two (they are so delicious they are usually eaten at once!)

NUTS AN' BOLTS

8 oz (225g) milk chocolate
1 tablespoon water
4 oz (100-125g) marshmallows

4 oz (100-125g) walnut pieces
1 dessertspoon cooking oil

Grease a small cake tin. Break the chocolate up into squares and put it into a small saucepan with the water. Heat it very, very gently, stirring all the time with a wooden spoon until it is melted and mixed. Take off the heat and pour half into the cake tin. Cut up the marshmallows and dot them all over the chocolate, together with the nuts. Pour the rest of the chocolate over the top. Put in a cool place to set, which usually takes about 8-10 hours (boring!) Cut up with a knife into odd shapes and eat.

ROSE PETAL JAM

1 pot

2 cups rose petals (push them
    right down into the cup when
    you measure them)
2 cups sugar

½ cup water
1 tablespoon lemon juice
1 tablespoon orange juice

In a saucepan over a gentle heat, dissolve the sugar in the water and the orange and lemon juice. Stir in the rose petals and, stirring all the time, keep on the heat for about 30 minutes or until all the petals have melted. Let it get cool and pour into a glass pot and cover.

FUDGE

makes about 1½ lb (775g)

1 lb (450g) soft brown sugar
2 oz (50g) butter or margarine
½ pint (150ml) milk
vanilla essence

Grease a rectangular tin about 8″ × 5″ (203 mm × 126 mm). Put the sugar, butter and milk into a saucepan and heat slowly until the sugar has dissolved. Turn up the heat and let the mixture boil. Let it boil for about 15 minutes, keep stirring it quite a lot or it will stick to the pan. Take the saucepan off the stove and beat the mixture hard with a wooden spoon until it is thick and fudgey. Pour it into the greased tin and leave it in a cool place to set.

CHOCOLATE TRUFFLES

makes about ½ lb (450g)

4 oz (100-125g) sweet biscuits
1 tablespoon golden syrup
1 tablespoon hot water
2 oz (50g) melted chocolate

1 oz (25g) margarine
1 teaspoon almond essence
chocolate 'hundreds and
   thousands'

With a rolling pin crush the biscuits to fine crumbs and put into a mixing bowl. Add the golden syrup and hot water. Melt the margarine and chocolate in a saucepan over a gentle heat. Add it to the biscuit mixture and beat well. Stir in the almond essence. When cool (about ¾ hour) divide the mixture into small balls and roll them in chocolate hundreds and thousands.

FOREN COOKIN'

FORENERS – FIRST OF ALL YOU GOTTA REMEMBER TO BE VERY CAREFUL ABOUT FORENERS 'COS THEY'RE ALL VERY CLEVER. F'r–INSTANCE FORENERS DON'T HAVE TO GO TO SCHOOL TO LEARN FRENCH AN' GERMAN AN' USELESS THINGS LIKE THAT 'COS THEY CAN SPEAK IT ANYWAY WHICH I DON'T THINK IS FAIR. THEY ALSO KNOW HOW TO DO LOTS OF FOREN COOKIN' WHICH IS PROBABLY 'COS THEY READ FOREN COOKIN' BOOKS.

CHINAMEN ARE MOSTLY YELLOWISH AN' DO LOTS OF CHINESE COOKIN AN' AMAZIN' THINGS WITH RICE..

CHINESE CHICKEN

4 helpings

left-over cold chicken cut into
bite-sized pieces
2 cloves garlic
1 green pepper

3 tablespoons soy sauce
3 tablespoons water
½ tablespoon sugar
1 tablespoon oil

Peel and cut up the garlic. Cut the top off the green pepper and scrape out the seeds. Rinse under the cold tap to make sure all the seeds are out. Cut up small. Heat the oil in a saucepan and gently fry the garlic and pepper. Add the water, soy sauce and sugar and stir it all around. Put in the chicken pieces and continue cooking very gently until the chicken is hot—about 15 minutes. This is very good eaten with rice.

FRENCHMEN ALL OWN LOTS OF
RESTRANTS WITH NAMES THAT ONLY
OTHER FRENCHMEN KNOW HOW TO
SAY AN' THEY'VE ALL GOT MENUS
THAT I BET NOT EVEN OUR FRENCH
TEACHER CAN READ....

CROQUE MONSIEUR (MISTER CROC)

bread
butter
cheese
slices of ham

Butter a slice of bread on one side, then cover with thin slices of cheese. Top this with a slice of ham, another slice of cheese and cover with a slice of bread to make a sandwich. Melt a small piece of butter in a frying pan over a low heat. Fry the sandwich slowly so that the cheese melts. Turn it over and fry the other side.

SAUTÉ POTATOES

4 helpings

3 large potatoes
salt and pepper
cooking oil or dripping

Wash and peel the potatoes. Chop them up into small cubes. Put a frying pan on the cooker and heat up some dripping or oil (just enough to cover the bottom of the pan when melted). Put the potato cubes in the pan and sprinkle salt and pepper on them. Keep on stirring them about so they don't stick to the bottom until they are brown and crispy.

FRENCH TOAST

makes 6 slices

1-2 eggs
½ teaspoon salt
sprinkle of pepper

½ pint (300ml) milk
slices of bread

Beat the eggs lightly in a big bowl, add the pepper and salt and the milk. Dip the slices of bread in this mixture. Heat a frying pan and put in a knob of butter. When it sizzles, drop each slice in one by one, cook for a few minutes, turn carefully over and cook the other side. Lovely with bacon and sausages or eaten on their own.

You can also make sweet French toast, by putting in sugar instead of salt and pepper. Cooked this way the slices are lovely with honey or golden syrup poured over.

ITALIANS ARE MOSTLY OPERA SINGERS AN' FOOTBALLERS AN' THE COUNTRYSIDE IS FULL OF SPAGETTI WHICH WE LERNT IN JOGRAPHY.

SPAGHETTI EGGS AN' BACON

1 lb (450g) spaghetti
4 rashers streaky bacon
3 eggs

¼ pint (150ml) single cream
salt and pepper
grated parmesan cheese

Nearly fill a large saucepan with cold water, add a tablespoon of salt and a tablespoon of cooking oil (this stops the spaghetti sticking together). Put it on the cooker over a high heat and wait until the water is boiling. Then gently push the spaghetti down into the water and stir it around with a wooden spoon. Watch it until it comes back to the boil and then turn the heat down until it is just simmering. Let it cook for about 12-15 minutes. (A good way to tell if it is cooked is to pull out one strand and throw it against the wall —if it sticks to the wall it's cooked!)

While the spaghetti is cooking, make the sauce.

In a heavy saucepan melt a tiny knob of butter. Cut the rind off the bacon rashers and chop each rasher up small. Cook them in the butter until they are crispy. Stir in the cream, salt and pepper and —only just—let it boil. Meanwhile break the eggs into a cup and beat them up. When the spaghetti is cooked, drain it off into a colander over the sink and stir in a knob of butter. Pour it into a large bowl. Stir in the cream and bacon mixture and mix it all around. Then pour in the eggs and stir it all about quickly so that it's thoroughly mixed. The heat of the spaghetti cooks the eggs. Serve with lots of grated parmesan cheese.

PIZZA

2 helpings

4 oz (100-125g) pastry
2 tomatoes
1 tablespoon oil
2 slices cheese (mozzarella from
the delicatessen is best)

4 fillets anchovy
sprinkle oregano or mixed
herbs

Turn on the oven to gas mark 6, electric 400°F (200°C). Roll out the
pastry to the size of a round flat baking tin. Grease the tin and lay
the pastry on it. Press down gently and trim off the spare bits round
the edge with a knife. Cut the tomatoes into thin slices and lay them
over the pastry. Sprinkle the oil and herbs over the top and cover
with the thinly sliced cheese. Decorate with the anchovy fillets and
bake near the top of the oven for 20 minutes.

SPANIARDS SPEND ALL THEIR TIME FIGHTIN' BULLS AN' DANCIN' WITH FLAMINGOES AN' EAT A LOT OF SPANISH OMLETTES.

SPANISH OMELETTE

2 helpings

2 potatoes
1 large onion
3 eggs

salt and pepper
4 tablespoons cooking oil

Wash and peel the potatoes and peel the onion. Cut the potatoes into
very thin slices (or grate them if you like). Cut the onion up very
small. Heat a frying pan over a gentle heat and pour in some of the
cooking oil. Tip in the potatoes and onions and fry them gently,
turning them over several times, until the potatoes are soft. Break
the eggs into a bowl, add the salt and pepper and beat them up with
a fork. Add the egg mixture to the potatoes and onions in the pan
and stir gently with a fork until it begins to set. Then with a spatula
or fish slice turn it all over and cook the other side. Cut it in half
and serve.

GREEKS ARE MOSTLY ANCIENT AN' PROBABLY SPOKE A LOT OF LATIN. THEY'RE VERY DANGEROUS IF THEY COME TO TEA 'COS THEY'RE QUITE LIKELY TO THROW PLATES AT EACH OTHER ALL THE TIME.

EASY MOUSSAKA

4-6 helpings

1 *lb* (450g) *minced beef*
1 *onion*
sprig of parsley
clove of garlic
salt and pepper

small tin of tomatoes
1 *plain yoghurt*
2 *eggs*
2 *tablespoons flour*
grated parmesan cheese

Turn on the oven to gas mark 4, electric 350°F (180°C). Heat an iron casserole dish on the cooker with a little oil in it. Put in the minced beef and stir it around with a fork. Peel and chop the onion and the garlic and wash and chop the parsley. Add them all to the meat. Stir for a few minutes, then add the salt and pepper and the tin of tomatoes. Let it simmer gently for about 15 minutes. Pour the yoghurt into a bowl and mix in the eggs, flour and parmesan cheese. Whisk it with an egg whisk until it is thick and creamy. Pour this carefully over the meat mixture. Put the dish in the middle of the oven and cook it for about an hour. The top should be golden brown.

WELSHMEN WEAR LEEKS, PICK DAFFODILS AN' EAT LOTS OF RABBITS.

WELSH RAREBIT

1 *slice of bread for each person (or 2 if they are hungry)*
4 *oz (100-125g) cheddar cheese*
1 *teaspoon mustard*
little top of the milk

Grate the cheese into a bowl and stir in the mustard and the top of the milk. Mix it all up until it is creamy. Toast the bread on one side only. Butter the untoasted side. Spread the cheese mixture on the buttered side and put it back under the grill until it is brown and bubbly.

CHEESY LEEKS

4 *helpings*

4 *leeks*
2 *oz (50g) cheddar cheese*
2 *oz (50g) breadcrumbs*
1 *oz (25g) butter*

Turn the oven on to gas mark 4, electric 350°F (180°C). Cut off the hairy roots and most of the green part of the leeks. Cut them in half lengthwise and wash them very carefully under the cold tap. Chop them up. Heat a saucepan on the top of the cooker with the butter in it, and when it has melted tip in the leeks. Keep stirring them around with a wooden spoon until they are beginning to get soft. Tip them all into an ovenproof dish. Grate the cheese and mix it up with the breadcrumbs and sprinkle this over the top of the leeks. Put the dish in the middle of the oven for about 40 minutes.

SCOTSMEN WEAR SKIRTS MOST OF THE TIME WHICH MUST BE PRETTY COLD CONSIDERIN' THEY GO HUNTIN' HAGGISES ALL OVER THE PLACE BLOWIN' BAG PIPES AT THEM TO KILL 'EM OFF — THEN THEY EAT 'EM.

SCOTCH PANCAKES

6 oz (175g) self-raising flour
1 tablespoon sugar
¾ teaspoon baking powder

4 helpings
¾ pint (150ml) milk
1 small egg

Make the batter in exactly the same way as for ordinary pancakes, only it will be much thicker (see page)   . Melt a knob of butter in a frying pan. Into the pan drop tablespoons of the batter so that they form small pools. You will probably be able to cook 2 or 3 at once. After a few minutes the pancakes will be golden brown underneath and well risen. Flip them over with a spatula or slice and cook the other side. They are lovely served at once, with lots of butter.

SHORTBREAD

Shortbread used to be the Scottish wedding cake, and if a girl put a piece under her pillow she was supposed to dream of the man she would marry. *GIRLS—I ASK YOU!* —

6 oz (175g) plain flour
3 oz (100-125g) soft butter
2 oz (50g) sugar

Turn on the oven to gas mark 3, electric 325°F (170°C). Sieve the flour into a bowl and rub in the butter with the tips of your fingers until the mixture looks like breadcrumbs. Pour in the sugar and knead it all together with your hands. Grease a 7-8 inch baking tin and push the shortbread into it—pressing it down well with your hands. Prick it all over with a fork. Put it in the centre of the oven for about 45 minutes. When you take it out, cut it into squares in the tin while still hot and then leave to get quite cool before taking it out.

DRINKIN'

GROWN-UPS SPEND MOST OF THEIR TIME DRINKIN' WINE AN' COCKTAILS AN' BEER AN' THINGS LIKE THAT BUT IF YOU ASK FOR A DRINK THEY TELL YOU TO GET SOME WATER OR A GLASS OF MILK. WHAT THEY DON'T SEEM TO REALISE IS WE LIKE DRINKIN' JUST AS MUCH AS THEY DO, ALTHOUGH JUST ABOUT EVERY-THING THEY DRINK IS REVOLTIN' SO IT'S A GOOD IDEA TO KNOW HOW TO MAKE YOUR OWN COCKTAILS AN' THINGS.

PINEAPPLE POLLY

4 helpings

1 *tin pineapple juice*
$\frac{1}{4}$ *teaspoon cinnamon*
$\frac{1}{2}$ *teaspoon ground cloves, ground nutmeg and all spice (mixed together)*

Pour the pineapple juice into a saucepan and add all the spices. Bring to the boil and let it simmer very gently for 20 minutes. Serve in mugs.

FROGS FIZZ

This makes a big jugful.

1 *can fizzy orange*
1 *can coca cola*
1 *can lemonade*
$\frac{1}{2}$ *bottle apple juice*

Mix all together in a jug and put in the fridge.

EXTRA SPECIAL LEMON SQUASH

2 *big bottles*
1½ *lb (675g) sugar*
4 *lemons*
1 *oz (25g) citric acid powder (bought from any chemist)*
2 *pints (1 litre) boiling water*

Put the sugar and citric acid powder into a large bowl. Grate the rind from the lemons and add it to the sugar. Pour the boiling water over all this and stir carefully until it is dissolved. Squeeze the juice from the lemons and add this too. Leave it to cool, then pour it into bottles and store in a cool place. It will keep for about a week. You should dilute it with water before you drink it.

Milk Shakes

makes 2

1 *pint (600ml) milk*
1 *egg*
1 *tablespoon sugar*

3 *tablespoons drinking*
  chocolate
blob of ice-cream

Put all the ingredients in a bowl and beat very hard with an egg whisk until they are all mixed and it is smooth and foamy. (Better still, whiz them up in the blender.) Pour into glasses and drink. For real luxury add a blob of ice-cream.

Instead of chocolate you can use coffee essence, or vanilla essence.

Iced Tea

4 *helpings*
3 *teabags*
water
½ *a lemon*
sugar

Put the teabags in a china jug or teapot. Fill it up with boiling water. After 5 minutes, fish out the teabags from the pot or jug. Add the juice of half a lemon. Add 3 tablespoons of sugar and stir. Put it in the fridge to get quite cold. Serve in glasses with an ice-cube.

MINT TEA

For two

In very hot countries like parts of Africa, this is almost the national drink, as, believe it or not, it's very refreshing on a hot day.

bunch of fresh mint
sugar
1 teabag

Wash the mint and stuff it into two tall glasses so that they are half full. Put a spoon in the glass (this will stop it cracking when you put the hot tea in). Make a very weak pot of tea. Leave it to stand for a few minutes, then fish out the teabag. Stir in plenty of sugar (about 2 tablespoons), then pour the tea over the mint in the glasses. Stir it all around and drink.

ICED COFFEE

milk
coffee essence ('Camp' coffee in a bottle)
sugar (if you want it sweet)

Take milk from the fridge—it must be cold—and pour into glasses. Add a tablespoon of liquid coffee for each glass, sugar, and stir.

GiNGER'S FiZz

milk from the fridge
ginger beer or ginger ale

Half fill a glass with cold milk. Then fill it to the top with ginger beer or ginger ale. A blob of ice-cream stirred in makes it extra special.

LiQuoRice WATER

makes 1 mugful

2 liquorice bootlaces
½ pint water

Heat a saucepan on the cooker with the water in and the liquorice broken into short lengths. Stir with a wooden spoon until it boils, then turn down the heat and continue stirring until the liquorice is all melted—about 5 minutes. Pour into a mug. Add sugar if you like things *very* sweet. Drink hot or cold.

SEESONAL COOKIN'

CHRISTMAS IS A GOOD TIME TO BE NICE TO EVERYONE SINCE THEY'RE ALWAYS WATCHIN' YOU TO SEE IF YOU'VE BEEN GOOD ENOUGH TO GIVE A PRESENT TO. S'POSE IF THEY THINK YOU'VE BEEN SPESHLY GOOD THEY GIVE YOU BIGGER PRESENTS.

SO ONE WAY OF PROVIN' YOU'RE SPESHLY GOOD IS TO GO AN' DO SOME OF THE CHRISTMAS COOKIN'

THINGS LIKE CHRISTMAS PUDDINS ARE PARTIC'LY GOOD 'COS YOU CAN MAKE 'EM IN THE MIDDLE OF SUMMER AN' KEEP REMINDIN' 'EM YOU DID IT, ALL THE TIME TILL CHRISMAS DAY.

THEN THERE'S EASTER AN' BONFIRE NITE AN' HALLOWE'EN AN' SPESHLY APRIL FOOLS DAY!

CHRISTMAS

CHRISTMAS BISCUITS

8 oz (225g) *flour*
4 oz (100-125g) *margarine*
4 oz (100-125g) *soft brown sugar*

1 *pinch ground ginger*
2 oz (50g) *treacle*
2 oz (50g) *golden syrup*

Turn on the oven to gas mark 5, electric 375°F (190°C). Sift the flour into a mixing bowl. Pour in everything else and mix it lightly together with your fingertips until you have a nice dough. Flour a board and roll the dough out gently with a rolling pin until it is about $\frac{1}{8}$ inch (3 mm) thick. You can cut it into any shapes you like—perhaps you have some cutter shapes, or you can make your own with thick card (a postcard would be fine). Decorate your biscuits with currants, chopped nuts or cherries or little silver balls. Put the biscuits on a greased baking sheet and put them in the middle of the oven for about 20 minutes. They should be light brown all over.

CHRISTMAS PUDDING

1 *lb* (450g) *seedless raisins*
12 *oz* (350g) *sultanas*
12 *oz* (350g) *currants*
4 *oz* (100-125g) *chopped candied peel*
2 *oz* (50g) *blanched almonds*
2 *oz* (50g)*flour*
2 *teaspoons mixed spice*
1 *teaspoon powdered cinnamon*

½ *teaspoon powdered nutmeg*
8 *oz* (225g) *sugar*
8 *oz* (225g) *fresh white breadcrumbs*
grated rind of 1 *lemon*
4 *oz* (100-125g) *suet*
4 *eggs*
¼ *pint* (150ml) *whisky or old ale or orange juice*

In a large mixing bowl, mix together all the raisins, sultanas, currants, peel and almonds. Sieve the flour and spices into the mixing bowl and add the sugar, breadcrumbs, rind and suet. Stir well. Add the eggs and the whisky, ale or orange juice. Stir and stir and stir, get all your friends to stir and have a wish. Have either one four-pint pudding basin or two two-pint basins well greased. Divide the mixture into the bowls, and cover each one with a circle of greased foil and then wrap each basin completely in a sheet of foil. Stand a large pan of water on the cooker and bring to the boil. Wearing oven gloves, lower the pudding in (you can only cook one at a time). The water must not come more than half way up the sides of the pudding. Boil for 6 hours. Every half an hour check that the water is high enough. If you need to, top up with boiling water from a kettle. When the time is up, take them out of the saucepan with oven gloves and leave to cool. Unwrap, and wrap up again in fresh foil and store in a cool dark place until Christmas. On Christmas Day boil again in the same way for another 3 hours.

MiNCE PiES

makes about 12

7 oz (200g) *plain flour*
½ *teaspoon salt*
4 oz (100-125g) *margarine*

water to mix
jar of mincemeat

Heat the oven to gas mark 7, electric 425°F (220°C). Sieve the flour and salt into a mixing bowl and add the margarine cut into small knobs. Rub it all together with your fingertips until it looks like breadcrumbs. Add the water—2 teaspoons at a time, and stir with a knife until the mixture is a nice firm dough. Put it on a floured board and roll it out thinly. With a round cutter, or the top of a tumbler, cut out circles of the dough. When you have cut as many as you can, squeeze up the dough, roll it out again and cut out some more. You will need two for each mince pie. Grease each section in a jam tart tin and line each one with a circle of pastry. Put a good tea-spoonful of mincemeat into each circle and brush round the edges with a little water. Put a pastry lid on each one and press down the edges firmly. Put in the middle of the oven for about 20 minutes. The pastry should be firm and golden. Take out of the oven and leave to cool for a few minutes before lifting them out. Sprinkle each one with castor sugar before serving.

EASTER

HOT CROSS SCONES
6 *helpings*

8 *oz (225g) self-raising flour*
1 *teaspoon baking powder*
1 *oz (25g) castor sugar*

2 *oz (50g) margarine or butter*
7 *tablespoons milk*
4 *oz (100-125g) sultanas*

Turn on the oven to gas mark 7, electric 425°F (220°C). Sieve the flour and baking powder into a mixing bowl. Stir in the sugar. Cut the margarine into small knobs and add to the flour. Rub it lightly between your fingers until it all looks like breadcrumbs. Add the sultanas. Pour in the milk and mix it all up with the blade of a knife until it is a soft dough. Roll it out with a rolling pin on a floured board until it is about ½ inch thick. With the rim of a glass cut circles of the dough and lift each one carefully on to a greased baking sheet. With a sharp knife mark a cross on each one. Put in the middle of the oven for about 12-15 minutes until they are a light golden colour.

EASTER BISCUITS

Follow the recipe for Christmas Biscuits and cut them into chicken shapes or egg shapes, using your home-made card stencils.

BONFIRE NIGHT
NOVEMBER 5th.

FIREWATER

3 *tablespoons lemon squash*
1 level *teaspoon powdered ginger*
2 *teaspoons sugar*
hot water

Put the lemon squash in a mug. Pour on the hot water, add the sugar and ginger and stir well.

HALLOWEEN
OctoBER 31st.

HALLOWEEN LANTERNS

Turnip or mangle wurzle or a pumpkin

Cut a circle out of the top (about 3 inches-7 cms). With a knife, loosen all the inside woody bits and scoop them out with a spoon. Leave it to dry out for an hour or so. With a sharp knife cut eyes, nose and mouth holes in one side. Wedge a nightlight or a small, fat candle in the bottom. Poke holes on either side at the top and tie some string through to hang the lantern up. Light the candle.

APRiL 1st.

APRiL FOOL'S DAY SURPRiSE

1 *small mint sweet*	*garlic powder*
little water	*ground cinnamon*
ground pepper	*ground ginger*
powdered mustard	*little ketchup*

Put a tiny drop of water on the sweet. Mix all the other ingredients together to make a paste. Roll the sweet in it and leave it in the fridge to set for about 15 minutes. **IT'S REVOLTiN'**

SHROVE TUESDAY

PANCAKES

4 *helpings*

1 *egg*	*some butter for frying*
3 *oz (75g) flour*	*a lemon*
¼ *pint (150ml) milk*	*a little sugar*

Make the pancake batter by sieving the flour into a mixing bowl. Make a well in the centre with your fist and break the egg into it. With a fork start beating the egg, pulling in a little flour from the sides of the bowl as you do so. Then add the milk slowly and carry on whisking until you have a smooth, creamy batter with no lumps of flour left. You can use it straight away but it's much better if you leave it to stand for an hour or so. Put a frying pan on the cooker and melt a knob of butter in it. Then pour in a ladleful of batter, tipping the frying pan from side to side so that the batter quite covers the bottom. Slide a fish slice gently under the pancake to see that it hasn't stuck and when the top side is set, shake the pan from side to side to loosen it. Then toss it in the air and it should (?!) land upside down and back in the pan. Cook that side for a few moments and then slide it out on to a plate. Squeeze some lemon juice over it, sprinkle it with sugar and fold it up. Put another knob of butter in the pan and start all over again.

HELPIN OUT

MOSTLY YOU'LL FIND IF YOU WANT
TO GO OUT AN' PLAY RED INDIANS AN'
THINGS THEY'LL SAY "WHY DON'T YOU
GO AN' COOK SOMETHING INSTEAD."

ONLY S'POSIN' YOU WANT TO COOK
SOMETHIN' AN' THEY'RE USIN' THE
KITCHEN THEY'LL SAY "WHY DON'T YOU
GO AN' DO YOUR HOMEWORK."

ONE WAY OF REACHIN' A COMPROMISE
WITH GROWN-UPS WHO NEVER REELY KNOW
WHAT THEY WANT YOU TO DO ('CEPT KEEP
OUT OF THE WAY) IS TO OFFER TO HELP
OUT WITH ALL OF THE TRIMMINGS AN'
THINGS THEY CAN EAT WITH THEIR BORIN'
OLD COOKIN'.

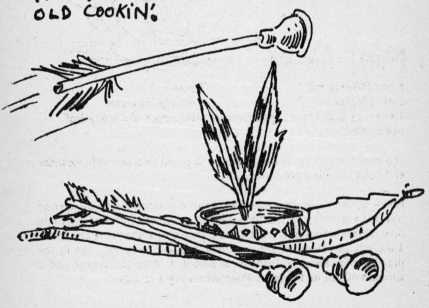

BREAD SAUCE

2 *tablespoons mint*
1 *tablespoon very hot water*
1 *teaspoon sugar*
1½ *tablespoons vinegar*

Strip the mint from the stalks and chop it finely on a chopping board. Put the sugar and water in a mug and stir until the sugar is dissolved. Add the mint and vinegar and stir well.

MINT SAUCE

¾ *pint (400ml) milk*
2 *oz (50g) butter*
3 *oz (75g) fresh white breadcrumbs*
small onion

2 *cloves*
1 *tablespoon cream*
salt, pepper and a bay leaf

(To make breadcrumbs, put pieces of bread into the coffee-grinder and whiz for a few seconds.)

Into a saucepan on the cooker put the milk, butter, onion, cloves and bay leaf and bring to the boil. Allow to simmer gently for a minute or two, remove from the cooker and leave to stand for 20 minutes. Take out the onion, cloves and bay leaf with a spoon. Stir in the breadcrumbs and put back on the cooker. Add the cream and a sprinkle of salt and pepper. Pour into a jug and serve.

GRASS SAUCE (FOR BACON)

2 *tablespoons chopped green grass*   1 *teaspoon sugar*
1 *tablespoon very hot water*   ½ *tablespoon vinegar*
6 *drops lemon juice*

Put the sugar and vinegar into a mug and add the water. Stir until the sugar has dissolved and add the lemon juice and the grass.

APPLE SAUCE

½ *lb (225g) cooking apples*
2 *tablespoons water*
knob of margarine
a little sugar

Peel, core and slice the apples. Put them in a saucepan with the water, and boil until they are soft, stirring so they don't stick to the pan. Take off the heat, sweeten with sugar to taste and stir in the butter.

FAVORITE COOKIN'

IF YOU CAN COOK ALL THE THINGS IN THIS BOOK LIKE A LOT OF PEEPLE CAN YOU COULD PROBABLY LIVE TO WELL OVER A HUNDRED BUT I THOUGHT I'D SAVE MY FAVORITES TO THE END..

KNICKERBOCKERGLORY

4-6 helpings

tin of peaches
block of ice cream
3 jellies—one red one green,
  one yellow

2 bananas
strawberries
a carton of double cream

Put a quarter of each jelly in separate dishes. Boil ¾ pint (400ml) of water in a saucepan and pour it equally on to each jelly. Leave it to set. Put a good spoonful of red jelly in each glass, then a spoonful of green jelly followed by ice cream. Lastly put in the yellow jelly topped with more ice cream. Slice the bananas and drain the juice from the peaches. Put bananas, ice cream, peaches and ice cream in layers to the top of the glass. Pour some cream on the very top and put one or two strawberries in the centre.

MERINGUES

6 helpings

2 eggs
4 oz (100-125g) castor sugar
oil
cream

Separate the eggs into yolks and whites. In a bowl, whisk the egg whites until they make little peaks when you lift the whisk out. Add half the sugar and whisk again. Very gently stir in the rest of the sugar with a fork. Turn on the oven to the lowest possible heat. Put a little oil on a baking sheet and spread it all over with a piece of kitchen towel. Spoon the egg and sugar mixture on to the sheet in little heaps. Put into the centre of the oven and leave for 2-3 hours. They don't really cook so much as dry out. Remove from the oven and place each one carefully on a wire rack to cool. When cool, sandwich them together in pairs with whipped cream in the middle.

TOFFEE APPLES

6 *hard eating apples*
6 *sticks (from ice lollies but wash
   them well)*

6 *oz (175g) sugar*
3 *fl oz (75ml) water*
1 *teaspoon lemon juice*

Wash the apples and take out any stalks. Push each one firmly on to
a stick. Put a saucepan on the cooker over a low heat, with the sugar
and water in it. Stir until the sugar dissolves, then add the lemon
juice. Turn up the heat and boil it fast, tipping the pan gently from
side to side, until it becomes caramel. Take the pan off the heat and
quickly turn each apple in the toffee until it is quite covered. Twirl
it over the pan until the toffee begins to set. Lightly oil a piece of
cooking foil and put in on a tray. Stand each apple on it upside down
and stand in a cool place until the toffee is completely set.

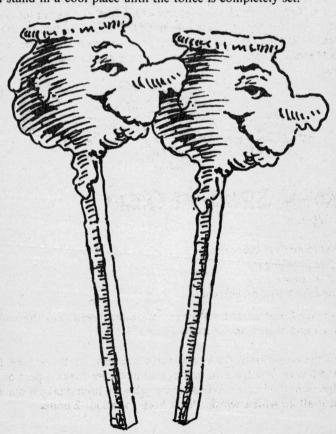

STRAWBERRY TARTS

1 oz (25g) *lard*
1 oz (25g) *margarine*
4 oz (100-125g) *plain flour*
½ *teaspoon salt*

cold water to mix
strawberries
double cream
castor sugar

Turn on the oven to gas mark 7, electric 425°F (220°C). Sieve the flour and salt into a mixing bowl. Cut up the fat into small knobs and rub it lightly into the flour with your fingertips until it looks like breadcrumbs. Add the water, two teaspoonsful at a time, till the mixture sticks together. With your hands, work it into a smooth firm dough. Flour a board and put the dough on it, roll it out until it is about a ¼ inch (5 mm) thick and cut circles out with the top of a tumbler. Grease each section in a jam tart tin and line each one with a circle of pastry. Prick the bottoms with a fork and put in the centre of the oven for about 12 minutes until a light golden brown colour. Take out of the oven and leave to cool. When cold, place one or two strawberries in each tart. Pour over a little cream and sprinkle with sugar.

BROWN BREAD ICE CREAM
6-8 helpings

1 *pint (600ml) double cream*
1 *tablespoon sugar*
vanilla essence
2 *handsful brown breadcrumbs*

(To make breadcrumbs, put pieces of brown bread into the coffee-grinder and switch on for a few seconds.)

Beat the cream until thick, add the sugar and vanilla essence. Stir in the brown breadcrumbs and put all in the ice-making part of the fridge or in the freezer. When frozen (about 3 hours) take it out and beat it all up with a whisk. Put it back for about 2 hours

GINGER BEER PLANTS AS PETS

WOT NOT MANY PEEPLE KNOW, IS THAT GINGER BEER PLANTS MAKE T'RIFFIC PETS. THEY'RE VERY QUIET AN' DON'T MAKE A LOT OF FUSS. SO LONG AS YOU KEEP FEEDIN' 'EM THEY'RE PERFECTLY HAPPY. BUT - YOU HAVE BEEN WARNED - THESE PLANTS ARE **DANGERUS!!**

REELY THEY ARE - IF YOR NOT VERY CAREFUL THEY GO **EXPLODING** ALL OVER THE PLACE BLOWIN' EVERYTHING UP, INJURIN' EVERYBODY IN SIGHT AN' MAKIN' A TERRIBLE MESS EVERYWHERE.

ON THE OTHER HAND YOU GOTTA START SOMEWHERE SO IF YOR THINKIN' OF BECOMIN' A LION TAMER WHEN YOU GROW UP I RECOMEND YOU START WITH GINGER BEER PLANTS.

A GINGER BEER PLANT

½ pint (300ml) tepid water
1 teaspoon sugar
1 oz (25g) yeast (from a good baker) or dried yeast

Mix the ingredients together thoroughly in a large jam or coffee jar. Every day for the next 7 days stir in:

½ teaspoon ground ginger
1 teaspoon sugar

In between stirring these in every day, leave the jar upright and still. (Always stir with a wooden spoon, as a metal one will do extraordinary things to the yeast!) Keep the top of the jar covered with a piece of kitchen towel.

After 1 week, strain off the liquid from the solid mass at the bottom of the jar—DO NOT THROW THIS AWAY! Remember, no metal, so use a nylon sieve. Next, take:

the juice of 2 lemons
2 lb (900g) sugar
6 pints (2½ litres) water

In a saucepan on the cooker heat 1 litre (approx 2 pints) of water and dissolve the sugar in it. Do not let it boil. Add this to the strained ginger liquid with the lemon juice and the rest of the water, and bottle.

Very important

1. When straining the plant, absolutely no solid matter must get through, so you may have to strain it more than once. A piece of clean muslin is very good, or even line the sieve with a piece of kitchen towel (although this is much slower).
2. When bottling, the bottles must have CORKS, *NEVER* screw caps. This is in case any yeast is still in the liquid. Pressure could build up inside the bottles. Corks will simply pop out, but if you use screw tops the bottles will explode and this is both extremely dangerous and *VERY* messy! Store your bottles where no harm can be done by flying corks. In the dark is best —like a cellar, attic or garden shed.
3. Bottles left for 3 weeks taste best.

Now you have made your ginger beer plant you can keep it going for ever. Just put *half* the brownish thick solid mass back in a clean jar and carry on adding the ginger and sugar every day.

HELPFUL HINTS

CHOP—e.g. an onion. Cut a slice off the top and bottom of the onion. Peel off all the brown skin. Cut the onion in half. Lay each half on a chopping board and cut downwards into slices. Holding the slices together cut them across and they will fall into small squares.

PINCH OF—as much as you can hold between your thumb and first finger.

SIMMER—only just boiling—so that the top of the mixture is just moving. Simmering water is filled with tiny bubbles.

BREAKING AN EGG—tap the egg firmly on the side of a dish or bowl and put your thumbnails in the crack. Then pull gently,. separating the two halves of the shell. Empty the egg into the bowl.

SEPARATING AN EGG—break an egg onto a plate, then get a small wine glass or an egg-cup and put it firmly over the yolk. Then holding the egg-cup or glass in place, pour off the white into a bowl. Now you have the white of the egg in a bowl, and the yolk on a plate.

HELPFUL HINTS

GREASING A TIN—get a piece of kitchen towel (paper) or a piece of greaseproof paper. If you use the towel, screw it up and put it on top of the cooking oil bottle. Then, holding the towel in place, turn the bottle upside down for a second. Then rub it over the baking tray or tin you are going to use. If you use the greaseproof paper, put a knob of butter or margarine (a small one) on the paper and rub that all over the tin. Or you can use a butter or margarine wrapper.

TELLING IF A CAKE IS DONE—open the oven, and put a sharp clean knife straight into the cake. If it is still clean when you pull it out the cake is done, but if it has some of the cake mixture stuck on it, it needs a few more minutes.

WHISK—put whatever needs whisking into a mixing bowl and beat it thoroughly with a fork or with a hand beater. If your mother has an electric mixer, ask her to show you how to use that, but be careful.

VALUABLE NOLEDGE FOR HAVIN' BONFIRES

TWIGS ETC. FOR GETTING FIRES STARTED:

VERY GOOD • Birch, Cedar, Cypress, Holly, Larch, Scots Pine, Silver Fir. Yew.

ALRITE • Ash, Beech, Hawthorn, Hazel. Lime, Laurel, Plane.

DREDFUL • Alder, Chestnut, Elder, Elm, Ivy, Oak, Poplar, Sycamore, Willow.

WOOD FOR SLOW BURNIN' BONFIRES:

VERY GOOD • Ash, Cypress, Holly, Laurel, Oak, Plane, Sycamore, Yew, Maple.

ALRITE • Alder, Beech, Birch, Cedar, Ivy, Larch, Lime Scots Pine, Silver Fir, Spruce, Willow.

DREDFUL • Chestnut, Elder, Hawthorn, Hazel, Elm, Poplar.

WOOD FOR QUICK BURNIN' BONFIRES:

VERY GOOD • Ash, Birch, Cedar, Cypress, Holly, Larch, Laurel. Scots Pine, Silver Fir, Spruce, Yew.

ALRITE • Beech, Sweet Chestnut, Hawthorn, Hazel, Ivy, Lime, Maple, Oak, Plane, Sycamore.

DREDFUL • Alder, Horse Chestnut, Elder, Elm, Poplar. Willow.

P.S. MAKE SURE YOU KNOW WHICH WAY THE WIND'S BLOWIN' BEFORE YOU START OR PEEPLE NEXT DOOR WILL ONLY COMPLANE 'BOUT THEIR FENCE BEIN' ALL BLACK AN' CHARRED. AN' THEIR WASHIN ALL GOIN' UP IN SMOKE...

GENERAL HINTS

MOST GROWN-UPS ARE LEFT WITH LOTS OF OLD TINS AND POTATO PEELINGS WHEN THEY'VE FINISHED COOKIN'.

YOU CAN PROBABLY GET TO DO ANYTHING YOU WANT TO FOR THE REST OF THE DAY IF YOU OFFER TO EMPTY THE RUBBISH FOR THEM. IT'S WORTH DOIN' COS SOMETIMES THEY DO STUPID THINGS LIKE THROW FOREN STAMPS AWAY IN THE BIN — COMPLETELY FORGETTIN' THAT YOU COLLEC 'EM.

IF YOR A BIT WORRIED ABOUT ANY OF
YOR COOKIN' TRY GIVIN' YOUR DOG A
BIT FIRST AN' SEE IF HE LIKES IT.
   DOGS LIKE MOST THINGS SO IT'S
PROBABLY GONE WRONG IF HE STARTS
BARKIN AT YOU.

EVEN THOUGH COOKIN'S TERRIBLY EASY
REELY GROWN-UPS ARE ALWAYS COMING
COMPLAININ' ABOUT HOW LONG IT TAKES
'EM AN' THEY'RE TRIFFICALLY PLEASED
IF YOU SAY SOMETHING NICE ABOUT
THEIR COOKIN.

INDEX

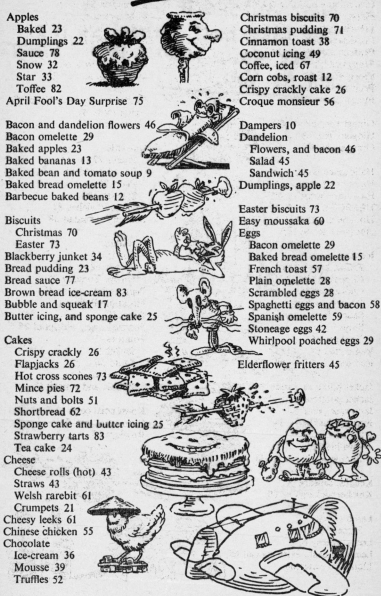

Frankfurters
  Pigs in blankets 10
Firewater 74
Five minute pudding 24
Flapjacks 26
French toast 57
Fried sandwiches 19
Fritters, elderflower 45
Frogs fizz 64
Frosty fruits 50
Fruit salad, orange 38
Fudge 52

Ginger beer plants 85
Ginger's fizz 68
Grass sauce 78

Hallowe'en lanterns 74
Hamburger drumsticks 8
Hawthorn surprise 45
HELPFUL HINTS 87
Hot cheese rolls 43
Hot cross scones 73

Ice-Cream
  Brown bread 83
  Chocolate 36
  Chocarina 23
  Knickerbockerglory 80
  Sauce, (marvellous) 38
  Snow 13
  Yoghurt 34
Iced coffee 67
Iced tea 65

Jacket potatoes, inside 9
Jacket potatoes, outside 17
Jam, rose petal 51
Junket, blackberry 34
Jelly
  Invalids 32
  Bunnies on the lawn 33

Kebabs, sausage 8
Knickerbockerglory 80

Lamb chops
  Parcel Post 18
Leeks, cheesy 61
Lemon squash, extra special 65
Liquorice water 68

Marshmallows, toasted 12
Marzipan dates 49
Meat-loaf 16
Meringues 81
Milk shakes 65
Mince pies 72
Mint sauce 77
Mint tea 67
Moussaka, easy 60
Mousse, chocolate 39

Nettles instead of cabbage 47
Nettle toast 47
Nutty toffee 50

Omelette
  Bacon 29
  Baked bread 15
  Plain 28
  Spanish 59
Open sandwiches 41
Orange fruit salad 38

Pancakes
  Potato 15
  Scotch 62
  Shrove Tuesday 75
Peppermint creams 49
Pineapple Polly 64
Pizza 59
Poached eggs, whirlpool 29
Potatoes
  Jacket 9
  Sauté 56
  Pancakes 15
  Bubble and squeak 17

Roast corn cobs 12
Rose petal jam 51
Rowleys 19

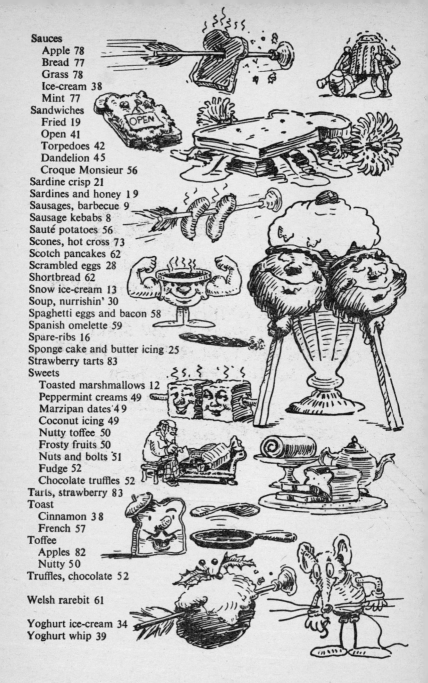

THE END

I WILLAM BROWN, TAKE NO
RESPONSIBILITY WHAT SO EVER FOR ANY OF
THE RECEPEES IN THIS BOOK.
IT'S NOT MY FAULT IF YOU START
GROANIN' ABOUT ALL OVER THE PLACE
WITH TERRIBLE FOOD
POISONIN'.

SIGNED

William Brown